Ricky the Rabbit and His Dancing Hands

A Story About Motor Stereotypies

Written and illustrated by LeeAnn Browett

For N.G.B., my very sweet and special hare.

Ricky the Rabbit has an interesting habit. He has hands that like to dance.

You may have noticed his hands moving and even stared or glanced.

When Ricky is excited, his hands and fingers start to wiggle.

Sometimes his feet join in too and jiggle.

If Ricky feels nervous or scared because he hears something go "Boo!"

his hands and feet might dance then too.

Ricky's dancing hands and feet show how he feels.

So don't worry about it. It's no big deal.

Ricky is a normal, healthy kid,

but his hands wouldn't stop dancing no matter what he did.

So if you see Ricky's hands start to move,

just ignore them and understand his body likes to groove.

It might be easier to understand too,

if we remember the things that happen to you.

Have you ever felt excited too

and your body did something you didn't expect it to do?

Have you ever let out a squeal when your mother makes your favorite meal?

Have you ever started to clap with joy when someone gives you your favorite toy?

Perhaps you have done a little dance when your friend comes over to play, by chance?

Well, Ricky's hands and feet also get clappy

when he feels excited, nervous, sad, and happy.

Ricky's dancing hands and feet have a name,

and saying the name almost feels like a game.

Let's try it now…"mo-tor-ster-e-o-ty-pies."

Try it a few more times and it will be a breeze!

I'm not sure what you have been told,

but you can't catch motor stereotypies like a cold.

Ricky's dancing hands are almost like a sneeze.

He doesn't make them dance on purpose, so don't ever tease.

Ricky and his friends love to play.

Jumping, singing, running, sliding, swinging, building, and pretending are all okay.

Remember Ricky's dancing hands just show how he feels.

Don't worry because it's really no big deal.

Ricky is our friend and a very sweet hare.

We know his movements are interesting and special. We understand. We care.

Ricky the Rabbit has hands that dance! Ricky has motor stereotypies and his hands move and groove when he feels excited, happy, nervous, and sad. Like all of us, Ricky the Rabbit wants to be accepted. Ricky needs his friends to understand him and care. This story will help children, parents, teachers, and friends understand motor stereotypies. Author-educator LeeAnn Browett has a child with non-autistic motor stereotypies and created the story of Ricky the Rabbit based on her own son's experiences.

Mo-

-tor

Ster-

-e-

-ty-

-pies

50183878R00017

Made in the USA
San Bernardino, CA
15 June 2017